# DCD Junkie

## C Interview Questions & Answers

*https://dcdjunkie.com*

# Contents

- Basics ............................................................................................................................ 2
- Bitwise ........................................................................................................................... 5
- Control Statements ..................................................................................................... 11
- Arrays & Pointers ........................................................................................................ 14
- Functions ..................................................................................................................... 17
- Command Line Argument ........................................................................................... 20
- Storage classes ........................................................................................................... 22
- Memory ........................................................................................................................ 24
- Structures & Unions .................................................................................................... 28
- Macros, typedef, enum ............................................................................................... 32
- Strings .......................................................................................................................... 34

## Basics

1. What are the compilation stages and its commands?
2. What is typecasting? What are the types of typecasting? Explain with example.
3. What is the format specifier for printing the address of a variable?
4. What are the types of errors are occurred in C?
5. What is code-optimization? What are advantages of code-optimization?
6. What are the types of qualifiers of a variable?

## Basics

## 1) What are the compilation stages and its commands?

The code which was written by a programmer is called a source code, that must be compiled into a machine code.

Compiler does this job, which happens in 4 stages.

There are 4 compilation stages.

1. **Pre-processor**

    Responsible for including header files, removing comments, replacing macros and for conditional compilation.

    Command: cc -E code.c -o code.i

2. **Translator**

    Responsible for Converting code into assembly code Checks for syntactical error

    Command: cc -S p1.i -o p1.s

3. **Assembler**

    Responsible for converting assembly code to machine code/pure binary code/op code (also known as object code)

    Command: cc -c p1.s -o p1.o

4. **Linker**

    Responsible for linking with libraries, adds OS related information as well.

    Command: cc p1.o

    The code which was written by a programmer is called a source code, that has to be compiled into a machine code.


## 2) What is typecasting? What are the types of typecasting? Explain with example.

Type casting is a way to temporarily change a type of data.

Typecasting can be done in two ways.

1. **Implicit type casting**: Compiler does it automatically.
   char ch ='R';

   int val = ch;

2. **Explicit type casting**: We are forcefully telling the compiler to do a typecast.
   double pi=3.1415;

   int val=(int)pi;

## 3) What is the format specifier for printing the address of a variable?

%p

## 4) What are the types of errors are occurred in C?

Errors/Bugs are mistakes(unintentionally) in the code that will not allow us to compile or run a code as expected.

Two types are errors occur,

**1) Compile time error**

- Compile time preprocessor error: Occurs in a preprocessor stage.
- Compile time translator error: Occurs in a translation stage.
- Compile time linker error: Occurs in a linker stage.

**2) Run Time error**

- Segmentation fault: Unauthorized memory access.
- Bus error: Accessing whose address is not present.

## 5) What is code-optimization? What are advantages of code-optimization?

It is a technique to improve the code, programmer also can do it, compiler also does it.

**Advantages**:

- To make code execution a little bit faster.
- To save some memory.

## 6) What are the types of qualifiers of a variable?

- **Size qualifier**: short, long, double.
- **Type qualifier**: const, volatile.
- **Storage class** qualifier: auto, register, static, extern.
- **Sign qualifier**: signed, unsigned.

## Bitwise

1. Write a program to set a bit, clear a bit, and complement a bit.
2. Write a one-line code to compare the two integer numbers using bitwise operator.
3. Write a program that converts Lower to Upper and Upper to Lower characters using bitwise.
4. Write a program to swap two integers using bitwise operators.
5. What are the values for the following?

## Bitwise

1) Write a program to set a bit, clear a bit, and complement a bit.

Three functions are defined in a code.

- int Set_Bit_Status(int,int);            ->    To set a bit
- int CLear_Bit_Status(int,int);          ->    To clear a bit
- int Complement_Bit_Status(int,int);     ->    To complement a bit

```c
#include<stdio.h>

void Print_Num_inBinary(int);
int Set_Bit_Status(int,int);
int CLear_Bit_Status(int,int);
int Complement_Bit_Status(int,int);

int main()
{
    int num,bit,option;
    printf("Enter a Number = ");
    scanf("%d",&num);

    Print_Num_inBinary(num);

    printf("Enter a bit(Position) to check = ");
    scanf("%d",&bit);

    if(bit >=0 && bit <= ((sizeof(int)*8)-1))
    {
        printf("Enter Option:\n1] Set 2] Clear 3] Complement\n");
        scanf("%d",&option);

        if(option == 1)
            num = Set_Bit_Status(num,bit);
        else if(option == 2)
            num = Clear_Bit_Status(num,bit);
        else if(option == 3)
            num = Complement_Bit_Status(num,bit);
        else
            printf("Invalid Option\n");

        printf("Now Number is = %d\n",num);
        Print_Num_inBinary(num);
    }
    else
    {
        printf("\nInvalid Bit Positon\n");
    }
    return 0;
}
```

```c
void Print_Num_inBinary(int n)
{
    int i;
    printf("\n%d Bit Binary Representation of a Number\n",sizeof(int)*8);
    for(i = ((sizeof(int)*8)-1);i >= 0;i--)
    {
        printf("%d",n >> i & 1);
        if(!(i%8))
            printf(" ");
    }
    printf("\n\n");
}

int Set_Bit_Status(int n,int b)
{
    n = n | 1 << b;
    return n;
}

int Clear_Bit_Status(int n,int b)
{
    n = n &~(1 << b);
    return n;
}

int Complement_Bit_Status(int n,int b)
{
    n = n ^ 1 << b;
    return n;
}
```

Output:

```
Enter a Number = 15

32 Bit Binary Representation of a Number
00000000 00000000 00000000 00001111
Enter a bit(Position) to check = 2
Enter Option:
1] Set 2] Clear 3] Complement
2
Now Number is = 11
Bit Binary Representation of a Number
00000000 00000000 00000000 00001011
```

2) Write a one-line code to compare the two integer numbers using bitwise operator.

```c
#include<stdio.h>

int Check_for_Equal_By_Bitwise(int,int);

enum Num_Status{IS_EQUAL,IS_NOT_EQUAL};

int main()
{
    int num1,num2,status;

    printf("Enter a Number_1 = ");
    scanf("%d",&num1);

    printf("Enter a Number_2 = ");
    scanf("%d",&num2);

    status = Check_for_Equal_By_Bitwise (num1,num2);

    if(status == IS_EQUAL)
            printf("%d and %d are equal\n",num1,num2);
    else
            printf("%d and %d are not equal\n",num1,num2);
    return 0;
}

int Check_for_Equal_By_Bitwise(int n1,int n2)
{
    if((n1 ^ n2) == 0)
            return IS_EQUAL;
    else
            return IS_NOT_EQUAL;
}
```

Output1:

```
Enter a Number_1 = 34
Enter a Number_2 = 34
34 and 34 are equal
```

Output2:

```
Enter a Number_1 = 34
Enter a Number_2 = 43
34  and 43 are not equal
```

3) Write a program that converts Lower to Upper and Upper to Lower characters using bitwise.

```c
#include<stdio.h>

char Change_Case(char);

int main()
{
    char ch;

    printf("Enter an Alphabet : ");
    scanf("%c",&ch);

    if((ch >= 'a' && ch <= 'z') || (ch >= 'A' && ch <= 'Z'))
    {
        ch = Change_Case(ch);
        printf("Changed Alphabet is = %c\n",ch);
    }
    else
    {
        printf("Not an Alphabet\n");
    }
    return 0;
}
char Change_Case(char c)
{
    return (c ^ (1 << 5));
}
```

Output1:

```
Enter an Alphabet : R
Changed Alphabet is = r
```

Output2:

```
Enter an Alphabet : r
Changed Alphabet is = R
```

4) Write a program to swap two integers using bitwise operators.

```c
#include<stdio.h>

int main()
{
    int num1,num2;

    printf("Enter a Number_1 = ");
    scanf("%d",&num1);

    printf("Enter a Number_2 = ");
    scanf("%d",&num2);

    printf("Before Swapping\nNum 1 = %d Num 2 = %d\n",num1,num2);

    if(num1 == num2)
    {
        printf("Same Data.\nNo Need to Swap\n");
        return 0;
    }

    num1 = num1 ^ num2;
    num2 = num1 ^ num2;
    num1 = num1 ^ num2;

    printf("After Swapping\nNum 1 = %d Num 2 = %d\n",num1,num2);

    return 0;
}
```

Output:

```
Enter a Number_1 = 10
Enter a Number_2 = 20

Before Swapping
Num 1 = 10 Num 2 = 20

After Swapping
Num 1 = 20 Num 2 = 10
```

5) What are the values for the following?

- sizeof 12345 : 4 bytes
- sizeof "12345" : 6 bytes

## Control Statements

1. Write a program to satisfy the if and else conditions.
2. What are the restrictions of switch cases?
3. What are minimum number of iterations for while loop?
4. What is volatile keyword?

1) Write a program to satisfy the if and else conditions.

```c
#include<stdio.h>

int main()
{
    int n1,n2;

    printf("Enter Number 1 = ");
    scanf("%d",&n1);

    printf("Enter Number 2 = ");
    scanf("%d",&n2);

    if(n1 == n2)
    {
            printf("Both are same\n");
            return 0;
    }

    if(n1 > n2)
            printf("%d is a bigger Number\n",n1);
    else
            printf("%d is a bigger Number\n",n2);
    return 0;
}
```

Output:

```
Enter Number 1 = 88676
Enter Number 2 = 3
88676 is a bigger Number
```

## 2) What are the restrictions of switch cases?

We can use only integer and character constants in switch case. We cannot use floats.

Any Statement in switch must be in any case (otherwise it will not be executed).

## 3) What are minimum number of iterations for while loop?

0 (Zero)

## 4) What is volatile keyword?

It is a type qualifier for a variable. It is applied to a variable when it is declared.

If a variable is declared as a volatile, we are informing the compiler that don`t apply any optimization for this variable, its value can be changed at any time.

Mostly it is used in embedded or RTOS projects.

## Arrays & Pointers

1. What are the differences between Arrays & Pointers?
2. What is the sizeof char pointer?
3. What is the difference between Array of pointer and Pointer to Array?
4. What is dangling pointer? How to avoid the dangling pointer?
5. What is void pointer, NULL pointer.

## Arrays & Pointers

1) What are the differences between Arrays & Pointers?

| Arrays | Pointers |
|---|---|
| Arrays are used to store values of the same data type. | Pointers are used to store addresses of a variable. |
| Array size is dependent on a number of its elements. (no. of element*size of single element). | Pointer size is fixed (environment dependent), for GCC 32 bit : 4 bytes. |
| Array cannot point to another variable. | Pointers can point to another variable. |

2) What is the sizeof char pointer?

4 bytes (for 64 bit environment it will be 8 bytes).

3) What is the difference between Array of pointer and Pointer to Array?

Array of pointers means it is an array whose elements are pointers. int *p[5];

So here, p is an array of 5 integer pointers.

p[0], p[1], p[2], p[3] and p[4] are integer pointers, each one can point to any integer,

like    int i=10,j=20,k=30;

p[0] = &i;

p[1] = &j;

p[2] = &k;

A pointer to an array means a pointer which is pointing to a array.

int (*p)[5];

p is a pointer pointing to an array of 5 integers.

int a[5] = {10,20,30,40,50};

int (*p)[5]; p = a;

value 10 can be retrieved by (*p)[0]

## 4) What is dangling pointer? How to avoid the dangling pointer?

If a pointer is pointing to a memory location that is deleted/freed, that pointer is called a dangling pointer.

To avoid this situation always initialize a pointer with NULL once it is freed.

    int *p = (int *)malloc(20);

    free(p);

    p = NULL; //no dangling now


pointer becomes dangling when,

- Accessing memory after memory is freed/deallocated.
- Trying to return the address of a local variable from a function (as scope of a local variable expires).

Note: It is purely a programmer`s mistake, programmers should take care handling pointers.


## 5) What is void pointer, NULL pointer.

Void pointer is also called as generic pointer, as it can point to any data type.

Void pointer is a pointer that points to some data location in memory storage, which does not have any specific data type.

It needs to be explicitly typecasted before dereferencing it.

NULL pointer: If a pointer is holding 0 (Zero) as ab address that pointer is called a NULL pointer.

Safest programming practice is while dealing with pointers if you are doing using it, make the memory free and make that pointer as a NULL pointer.

## Functions

1. What is Function? What are the advantages?
2. What is the difference between Call by Value & Call by reference?
3. What is static function?
4. What is Function Pointer?
5. What is the recursion function? What are the advantages and disadvantages?
6. What is a call back function? Give one example of it.

## 1) What is Function? What are the advantages?

A function is a small separate block of code that does some specific tasks.

A set of instructions that are put together to do some tasks.

Building block of a program is a function.

Functions are of two types.
1. Pre-defined functions: Compiler defined functions/library functions
2. User defined function: Functions that we have defined as per our needs.

**Advantages:**

- Code looks cleaner.
- Modularity can be achieved.
- Debugging becomes easy.

## 2) What is the difference between Call by Value & Call by reference?

In coding, function can be called two ways.
1. Call by value
2. Call by reference

Call by value copies the data only, so it won't affect the actual argument.

change_value(x);

Call by reference copies the address of an argument so the changes made here will affect the passed arguments. No copy is done here, so it saves the memory.

change_value(&x);

## 3) What is static function?

A static function is just the same as a normal function, it just means that it can be accessed in another file.

By default, function has a global scope, any other file can use it. Static function`s scope is limited to the file where it is defined. Static function is secured as no other file can use it.

## 4) What is Function Pointer?

Function pointer is a pointer that can point to a function.

It can be used to call different functions with the same function pointer (arguments should be the same).

```c
int sum(int a,int b)
{
        return a+b;
}

int (*fp)(int, int) = sum;
int ans = fp(10,20); //ans = 30

int sub(int a,int b)
{
        return a-b;
}
int (*fp)(int, int) = sub;
int ans = fp(20,10); //ans = 10
```

## 5) What is the recursion function? What are the advantages and disadvantages?

Recursive/Recursion functions are the function that calls itself.

Always be careful while using a recursive function, because if no proper exit condition is provided, it will go into an infinite loop (will crash when RAM is filled with stack frames).

**Advantages:**

- Big algorithms can be solved easily Few lines of code needed.

**Disadvantages:**

- Recursive functions slower.
- It occupies more memory.

## 6) What is a call back function? Give one example of it.

The functions which are taking one of its argument as a function pointer are called call back functions.

```c
int fun(int i, int j, int(*p)(int, int))
{
        return((*p)(i,j));
}
```

fun is a callback function in above code.

## Command Line Argument

1. What is command line arguments? What is the use of that?
2. By default, Command line Arguments are treated as.

## Command Line Argument

1) What is command line arguments? What is the use of that?

It is an argument/parameter that is given while putting the code into the run.

Used when you do not want to give input at run time, but you want to give input to a code at load time.

For this main function declaration would be like,

```
int main(int argc, char *argv[])
```

**Where**,

argc holds the number of arguments (including executable file).

argv holds the base address of an array of a pointer.

It is a pointer array. which holds the pointers of type character (which points to arguments passed). Arguments are separated with space.

Each passed argument is treated as a string. For Examples:

./a.out arg1 arg2 arg3....

2) By default, Command line Arguments are treated as.

Strings

## Storage classes

1. Explain the 4 specifications   1) Scope 2) lifetime 3) Default Value 4) Storage of all storage classes.
2. Can we declare register variable as global?
3. Can we access the addresses of registers?
4. What is the default storage class for any function?

1) Explain the 4 specifications   1) Scope 2) lifetime 3) Default Value  4) Storage of all storage classes.

**Auto**

- Scope          :     Within block
- Lifetime       :     End of block
- Default value  :     Garbage
- Storage        :     Stack frame

**Static**

- Scope          :     Within a function if local static, within a file is global static
- Lifetime       :     Till end of the program execution
- Default Value  :     0 (Zero)
- Storage        :     Data Segment

**Register**

- Scope          :     Within block
- Lifetime       :     End of block
- Default value  :     Garbage
- Storage        :     CPU register, if registers not available then stack frame

**Extern**

- Scope          :     Multiple files
- Lifetime       :     Till end of the program execution
- Default Value  :     0 (Zero)
- Storage        :     Data Segment

2) Can we declare register variable as global?

NO.

3) Can we access the addresses of registers?

NO.

Compiler may give an error or warning depending upon the compiler you have used.

4) What is the default storage class for any function?

Extern

# Memory

1. What is the difference between malloc & calloc?
2. What is the return type of malloc function?
3. What is the use of realloc function?
4. Write a program to allocate memory dynamically without using malloc and calloc functions.
5. What is memory leak? How to avoid it?
6. Write a program to free the dynamic memory allocation without using free() function.

## 1) What is the difference between malloc & calloc?

Both are useful for allocating memory at run time. Both return the starting address of a dynamically allocated memory.

| Malloc | calloc |
|---|---|
| The name malloc stands for memory allocation. | The name calloc stands for contiguous allocation. |
| malloc() takes one argument that is, number of bytes. | calloc() take two argument number of blocks and size of each block. |
| void *malloc(size_t n); | void *calloc(size_t n, size_t size); |
| Malloc allocates n bytes of memory, if allocation is successful then a void pointer to an allocated memory is returned, in case of failure NULL is returned. | calloc allocates contiguous blocks of memory and also initializes allocated memory to zero, in case of failure NULL is returned. |
| Malloc is faster. | Calloc is slower since it does initialize memory with 0. |

## 2) What is the return type of malloc function?

It returns the base address of a dynamically allocated memory if it can allocate the memory, NULL is return in case of failure.

## 3) What is the use of realloc function?

It try to resizes the memory allocated by malloc/calloc, and returns the pointer to newly allocated memory in case of successful allocation.

```
void *realloc(void *ptr, size_t size);
```

It will return NULL in case of failure.

So let us say previously you allocated 20 bytes of memory using malloc/calloc and now you reallocate it to 40 bytes, so it checks whether continuous 40 bytes are available or not, if it is available then it just extend the same memory location to use 40 bytes if not then it finds continuous 40 bytes available memory location, allocates it and returns the pointer to a newly allocated memory.

4) Write a program to allocate memory dynamically without using malloc and calloc functions.

```c
#include<stdio.h>
#include<stdlib.h>

int main()
{
    int *ip = NULL;

    ip = (int*)realloc(ip,4);
    *ip = 10;

    printf("Address of ip=%p and data=%d\n",ip,*ip);

    return 0;
}
```

Output:

```
Address of ip=0x17a9010 and data=10
```

5) What is memory leak? How to avoid it?

If we lose the base address of a dynamically allocated memory that memory becomes weak, because we cannot free that memory.

**For example:**

```
int *p = (int*)malloc(20); Here 20 bytes are allocated,
p = (int*)malloc(40);
```

Now again with the same pointer we are allocating 40 bytes, so that previously allocated memory is leaked, it cannot be freed as we lose its base address.

**To avoid memory leak**,
- Use another pointer for new allocation.
- Free the memory after you are done using it.

6) Write a program to free the dynamic memory allocation without using free() function.

```c
#include <stdio.h>
#include <stdlib.h>

int main()
{
    int *ip = NULL;

    ip = (int*)malloc(4);
    *ip = 25;
    printf("Address of ip=%p and data=%d\n",ip,*ip);

    printf("<--Free the memory-->\n");
    ip = (int*)realloc(ip,0);

    printf("Address of ip=%p\n",ip);

    return 0;
}
```

Output:

```
Address of ip=0x12e6010 and data=25
<--Free the memory-->
Address of ip=(nil)
```

# Structures & Unions

1. What is structure? What are differences between Arrays and Structures?
2. When is the memory is created to the structure?
3. What is structure padding? How to avoid structure padding?
4. Write a program to find the sizeof structure without using sizeof operator?
5. What is self-referential structure?
6. What is union? What are the advantages & disadvantages of using a union?
7. What are differences between Structure and Union?

## 1) What is structure? What are differences between Arrays and Structures?

Structure is a collection of different types of data stored in a contiguous memory location.

It is a secondary data type.

Size of a structure is a total size needed for each member of a structure.

```
Struct A
{
    int a;
    char b;
    float f;
};
```

| Array | Structure |
|---|---|
| Array is a collection of same data type stored in a contiguous memory location. | Structure is a collection of different data types stored in a contiguous memory location. |
| Array uses [] subscript operators. | Structure uses dot (.) operators. |
| Bit files are not there in array. | Bit field is possible with structure. |
| Size is fixed for array, size of an element multiplied by number of elements. | Structure size is not fixed as the number of elements are not fixed. |

## 2) When is the memory is created to the structure?

For structure memory is not allocated when you declare it, when you create a variable for that structure then only memory is allocated for it.

## 3) What is structure padding? How to avoid structure padding?

Allocating memory for a structure variable more than the required memory is called a structure padding. The extra bytes which are allocated are called holes in a structure.

To avoid structure padding,

- put all the smaller size variables at one side. Use #pragma pack directive.
- Memory alignment should be multiple of 2.

    #pragma pack 2

4) Write a program to find the sizeof structure without using sizeof operator?

```
#include <stdio.h>

int main()
{
    struct A
    {
        int i;
        char c;
        float f;
    };

    struct A *p1=NULL;

    p1++;
    printf("Size of a strcture : %d\n",p1);

    return 0;
}

Size of a strcture : 12
```

5) What is self-referential structure?

A structure which has one of more pointers that points to the same type of structure as their member are called self-referential structure.

```
struct A
{
    int i;
    char c;
    struct A* ptr;
};
```

6) What is union? What are the advantages & disadvantages of using a union?

Union is a collection of different types of data stored in the same memory location.

Which member needs highest memory that much memory is allocated for a union.

```
union A
{
    int i;
    char c;
    float f;
};
```

**Advantages:**

- It saves the memory.
- Like for similar variable structure takes 12 bytes, here only 4 bytes are needed for a union.

Disadvantages:

- It shares common memory.
- Only one data is accessible at a given time.
- Changing data of one variable/member of a structure affects rest of all member due to same memory.


7) What are differences between Structure and Union?

| Structure | Union |
| --- | --- |
| The size of a structure is greater or equal to the sum of sizes of its all members. | The size of a union is the size of its largest member. |
| For each element of a structure memory is different. | The same memory is shared between each element of a union. |
| In a structure any variable can be accessed at a time. | Only one member can be accessed at a time. |
| Several members can be initialized at once. | only one member can be uninitialized at a given time. |

## Macros, typedef, enum

1. What is enum? What are the advantages?
2. What is typedef? What are the advantages?
3. What is FILE in C? What is the size of that?
4. What are the differences between macros and functions?
5. What is the difference between #define and typedef?

## 1) What is enum? What are the advantages?

Enumeration is a user define datatype. We can put a name for an integer constant with the help of enum.

**Advantages:**

- Code readability improves.
- Easy to maintain a code.

## 2) What is typedef? What are the advantages?

Using a typedef we can put an alias name or another name to the existing type.

**Syntax**:

typedef old_dataType_name new_name;

**Advantages**:

- It improved readability
- Easy to use.

## 3) What is FILE in C? What is the size of that?

FILE is a structure pointer in C. its size is of 4 bytes.

## 4) What are the differences between macros and functions?

| macros | functions |
| --- | --- |
| Macro body replacement is done in pre-processor stage. | Function is compiled. |
| Using macro increases code length. | Code length is unaffected. |
| Execution is faster. | Slower. |
| For small code it is used. | For larger code it is used. |

## 5) What is the difference between #define and typedef?

| typedef | #define |
| --- | --- |
| typedef is used to give a different name to a data type only. | #define directive can be used with types and for values as well. |
| typedef is done at translation stage. | #define is done at the pre-processor stage. |
| typedef is terminated with ;(semicolon). | #define should not have ;(semicolon) at the end. |
| typedef gives a new name | #define replaces. |

## Strings

1. What are the return values of strcmp function?
2. Write a one-line code to copy string into destination.
3. What is the difference between strcpy and memcpy?
4. What does Header file and Libraries contain?

1) What are the return values of strcmp function?

Strcmp function used to compare two strings.

The comparison is done using unsigned characters.

```
int strcmp(const char *s1, const char *s2);
```

The return value from strcmp is,

- 0, if the s1 and s2 are equal.
- A negative value if s1 is less than s2.
- A positive value if s1 is greater than s2.

2) Write a one-line code to copy string into destination.

```
#include <stdio.h>
#include<stdlib.h>

int main()
{
    char *s1 = "C_Coding",*s2=NULL;

    s2 = (char*)malloc(10);

    while(*s2++ = *s1++);

    printf("s2=%s\n",s2-9);

    return 0;
}
```

3) What is the difference between strcpy and memcpy?

| strcpy | memcpy |
|---|---|
| strcpy used to copy source string to destination string. | memcpy used to copy a specified number of bytes from one memory to another memory. |
| char *strcpy(char *dst, const char *src); | void* memcpy(void *restrict out, const void *restrict in, size_t n); |

## 4) What does Header file and Libraries contain?

Header file contains declaration of pre-defined functions, macro definitions, global variable declarations, struct, union, enum etc.

Library contains definitions of pre-defined functions like printf, scanf etc.

It contains .o file(object files)

https://dcdjunkie.com

Hi all, Hope this question & answers will help you in interview. I have answered the questions very briefly, you can search more about these topics.

Checkout some cool programs on https://dcdjunkie.com and on YouTube channel dcdjunkie, where I have made a C code of Tic Tac Toe game.

# DCD Junkie

 https://www.youtube.com/c/Dcdjunkie

 https://www.facebook.com/dcdjunkie

 https://www.instagram.com/code.dcd/

 https://twitter.com/DcdJunkie

rohit.eceng@gmail.com

www.ingramcontent.com/pod-product-compliance
Lightning Source LLC
Chambersburg PA
CBHW080437220526
45465CB00009B/3328